GERALD OF WALES

Author and translator
Robert M. Morris

Cardiff
University of Wales Press
1987

© Crown copyright, 1986

British Library Cataloguing in Publication Data

Morris, Robert M.
  Gerald of Wales.
  1. Giraldis, Cambrensis — Juvenile literature
  2. Historians — Wales — Biography —
  Juvenile literature
  I. Title II. Gyrfa Gerallt. *English*
  942.9'0072024 DA209.G5

  ISBN 0-7083-0968-2

All rights reserved. No part of this book may be reproduced, stored in a retrieval system, or transmitted, in any form or by any means, electronic, mechanical, photocopying, recording or otherwise, without clearance from the University of Wales Press, 6 Gwennyth Street, Cathays, Cardiff CF2 4YD.

ACKNOWLEDGEMENTS

The publishers would like to thank the following for permission to reproduce photographs and for their assistance.

BBC Hulton Picture Library: frontispiece, 3(A), 3(B), 3(C), 8(B), 11(B), 18(A)

The Mansell Collection Ltd: 3(D), 3(E), 20(E)

Anne Mainman: 4(F)

Royal Commission on Ancient and Historical Monuments in Wales: 7(D), 15(D), 19(C)

Eric Hall: 7(E), 15(F), 16(K), 17(M), 17(N)

Trinity College, Cambridge: 9(D)

National Library of Wales: 9(E)

The British Library: 10(G)

Cardiff City Council: 11(C)

Welsh Folk Museum: 12(F)

Elfed Williams: 16(I)

Conway Library, Courtauld Institute of Art; Maurice H. Ridgway: 18(B)

Cadw, Welsh Historic Monuments: 21(H)

Biblioteca Apostolica Vaticana: 22(C)

Ian Rolls: 24(F)

CONTENTS

Gerald's Age — A Survey 2
1. Introduction 3
2. Home and Family 5
3. The Student and the Priest 8
4. Fame and No Fortune 11
5. The Journey through Wales 13
6. Triumph and Defeat 18
7. The Twilight Years 22
8. Glossary 24

TIME-CHART OF MAIN EVENTS

1164 Henry II flees from the Berwyn
1169 Normans invade Ireland
1170 Thomas à Beckett murdered
1176 Cardigan Eisteddfod
1187 Turks invade Jerusalem
1188 Gerald campaigns for the crusades
1189 The King dies in France
1193 Richard III missing in Austria
1197 The Lord Rhys dies
1215 John signs Magna Carter
1223 Gerald of Wales dies

It was not possible to trace the originator of every picture or source contained in this book.

This book is based on an original Welsh title, *Gyrfa Gerallt*.

Printed in Wales by Graham Harcourt (Printers) Ltd., Swansea.

SYLVESTER GIRALDUS CAMBRENSIS.

GERALD'S AGE: A SURVEY

THE POPES IN ROME

Honorius II	1124-1130
Innocent II	1130-1143
Celestine II	1143-1144
Lucius II	1144-1145
Eugenius III	1145-1153
Anastasius IV	1153-1154
Adrian IV	1155-1159
Alexander III	1159-1181
Lucius III	1181-1185
Urban III	1185-1187
Gregorius VIII	1187
Clement III	1187-1191
Celestine III	1191-1198
Innocent III	1198-1216
Honorius III	1216-1227

BISHOPS OF ST DAVID'S

Bernard	1116-1147
David Fitzgerald	1147-1176
Peter de Leia	1176-1198
Gerald of Wales's Campaign	1198-1203
Geoffrey of Henlaw	1203-1215
Iorwerth	1215-1229

KINGS OF ENGLAND

Stephen	1135-1154
Henry II	1154-1189
Richard I	1189-1199
John	1199-1216
Henry III	1216-1272

LORDS OF DEHEUBARTH

Cadell ap Gruffudd	
Maredudd ap Gruffudd	} 1137-1155
Rhys ap Gruffudd	
Rhys ap Gruffudd (Lord Rhys)	1155-1197
Civil War	1197-1201
Maelgwyn ap Rhys	} 1201-1231
Rhys Grug	

THE PRINCES OF GWYNEDD

Owain Gwynedd	1137-1170
Civil War	1170-1174
Rhodri ap Owain	
Dafydd ap Owain	} 1174-1194
Gruffudd ap Cynan	
Maredudd ap Cynan	
Gruffudd ap Cynan	} 1194-1201
Maredudd ap Cynan	
Llywelyn ap Iorwerth	
Llywelyn ap Iorwerth	1201-1240

ARCHBISHOPS OF CANTERBURY

Theobald	1139-1162
Thomas à Becket	1162-1170
Richard	1174-1185
Baldwin	1185-1190
Hubert Walter	1193-1205
Stephen Langton	1207-1228

1. INTRODUCTION

Look at the series of pictures A – E, and the captions beneath them.

A Henry II, King of England from 1154 to 1189.

B Richard I, King of England from 1189 to 1199: he fought in the Crusades in the East.

C King John (1199-1216), as he was shown in a manuscript from the Middle Ages.

D Pope Innocent III (1198-1216).

E Stephen Langton, Archbishop of Canterbury (1207-1228).

F Rhys ap Gruffudd, Lord of Deheubarth (1155-1197), at the first eisteddfod in Cardigan, 1176.

These pictures show men of the Middle Ages — three kings, one prince, a pope and an archbishop. The kings ruled over England, much of Wales and large areas of France too. The archbishop was the leader of the Church in the kingdom, and the pope was the head of the Roman Catholic Church throughout Europe. The prince was also a blood relative of the hero of this book.

This book is not about these great men, but about another man who knew them all personally (as well as two other archbishops not mentioned here). He was a Welshman, related to a family of Welsh princes. He did official work for the three kings shown in pictures A, B and C; he was a prominent man of the Church and, above all, the author of many interesting books.

In an age when few people could read or write at all, this man's books drew a clear and colourful picture of the important people of the time, of Wales, her land and people, and of the Church.

This man was called Gerald of Wales, and in this book you will look at his career and his life-story through his own eyes. But before we join Gerald himself, here is a chance for you to judge the importance of the man and his book from some things that were said about him in his own time and later:

G As long as Wales survives, he will be praised for his good work by the authors of the chronicles and in the songs of the bards.

Llywelyn Fawr, Prince of Gwynedd (1201-1240)

H Our Wales often wages great wars against England, but never anything as great and serious as has been done in our time by the bishop-elect of St David's [Gerald]. He has not ceased to attack and trouble the king, archbishop, and the whole clergy and people of England as well, with long and sustained efforts, for the honour of Wales.

(Gwenwynwyn, Prince of Powys, trans. Robert Bartlett)

I One of the most learned of men in a learned age ... He mastered more languages than most of the men of his age, and examined them in a scientific way that was typical of even fewer men of his time.

Edward A. Freeman (historian, 1823-1892)

J His Welsh blood was thin, and yet his sympathies with Wales were hateful to his enemies and an obstacle to his getting on in the world. He was a good companion and a lively storyteller, but his words sometimes cut to the quick ... His observant eye, his retentive memory, his ability to note interesting and relevant features, as well as his fluent prose, has given us books incomparable in their descriptive power and priceless as historical documents.

A. H. Williams (historian), 1948

2. HOME AND FAMILY

If Gerald of Wales had heard somebody call out 'Hey, Gerald! Gerald of Wales!', or 'Gerallt! Gerallt Gymro!', he probably would have had no idea that his name was being called. It is unlikely that he could speak much Welsh or English, and he was certainly not called 'Gerald', or 'Gerallt' either. He had been christened Sylvester Giraldus de Barri, around the year 1146. His family was part Norman —landowners and knights — and part Welsh — the family of one of the famous princes of Wales.

1. Look at the map of Wales A as it was at the end of the twelfth Century, when Gerald was a middle-aged man. Who then ruled most of south-west Wales? In what county is most of that region today?

Gerald's parents were William de Barri, a Norman knight, and Angharad. Gerald's most influential and interesting relatives were on his mother's side of the family: and it was in this branch of his family that he took the most pride. Angharad was the daughter of Gerald de Windsor and his wife Nest. Gerald had been one of King Henry I's important officials, and he was made Constable of Pembroke Castle. Nest was the daughter of the King of Deheubarth, Rhys ap Tewdwr, at a time when most of Wales was divided into a number of independent kingdoms. So Gerald was related to a Welsh royal family, and he was proud of it. Yet he was proud of his Norman relations too — the tough, daring knights who had invaded and conquered England and large areas of south Wales since William the Conqueror won the English crown in 1066. The **family tree**, or genealogy B will show you who Gerald's relatives were:

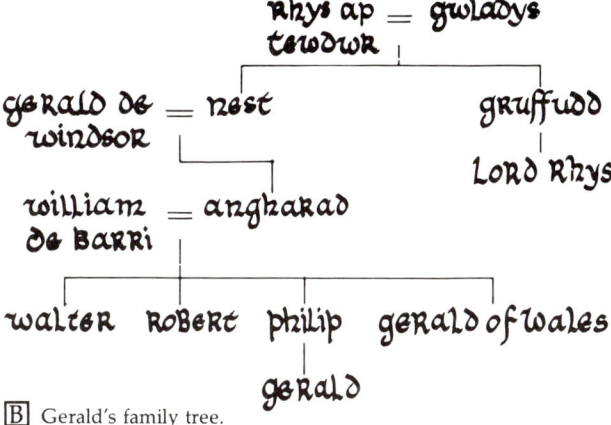

B Gerald's family tree.

THE YOUNG GERALD

Gerald was born and brought up in Manorbier Castle near Pembroke, Dyfed. This is his own description of his childhood home: C

C Of all the land of Wales Dyfed, with seven cantrefs, is the most beautiful and desirable; and of Dyfed, Pembroke; and of Pembroke the land described above Manorbier. It follows, therefore, that this spot is the most delightful in all Wales.

(Gerald of Wales, *Itinerarium Kambriae*, trans. Lewis Thorpe)

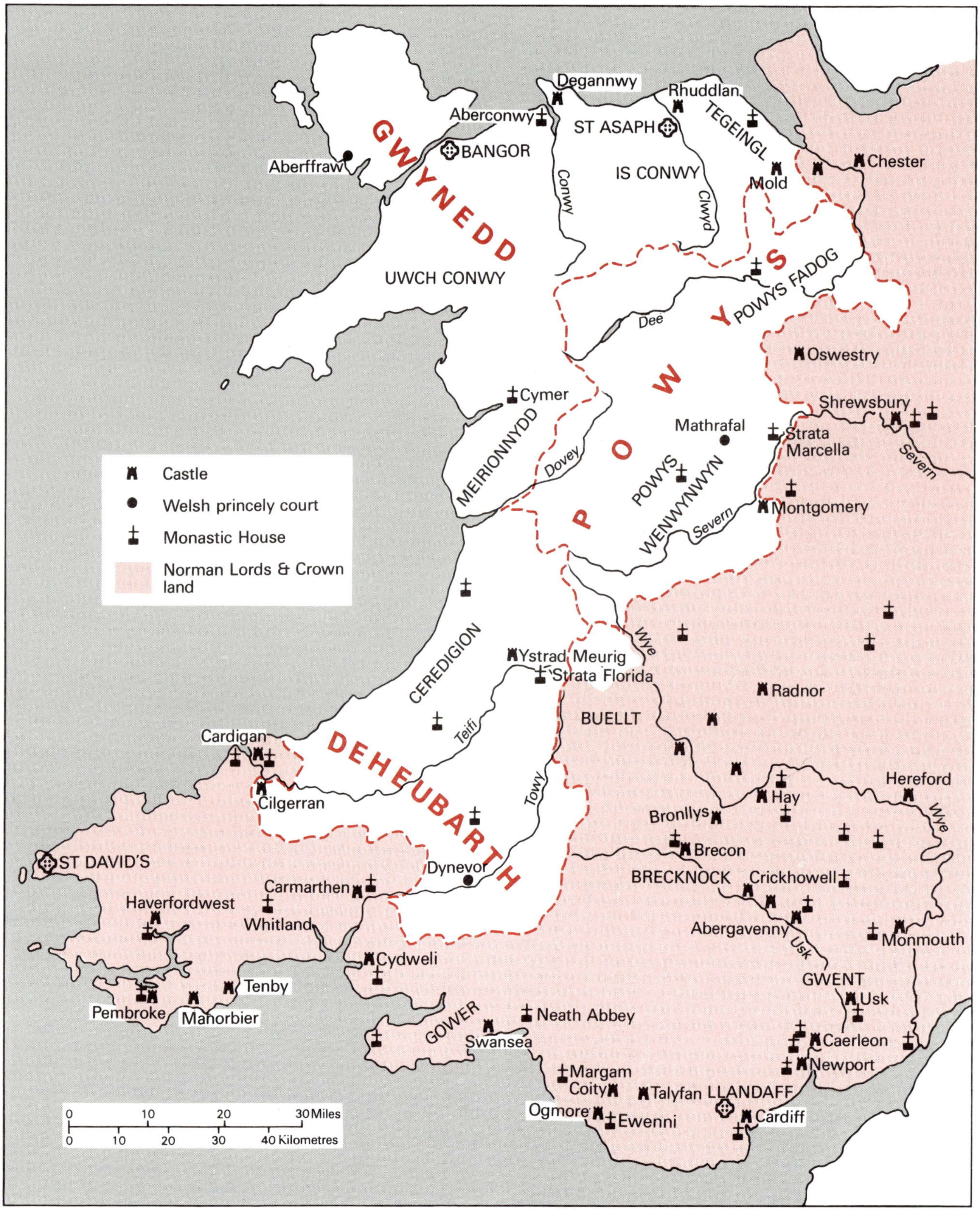

GWYNEDD
Degannwy
Rhuddlan
Aberconwy
ST ASAPH
TEGEINGL
Aberffraw
BANGOR
IS CONWY
Conwy
Clwyd
Mold
Chester
UWCH CONWY
POWYS
POWYS FADOG
Dee
Oswestry
Cymer
Shrewsbury
Mathrafal
Strata Marcella
MEIRIONNYDD
Dovey
POWYS WENWYNWYN
Severn
Montgomery
Castle
Welsh princely court
Monastic House
Norman Lords & Crown land
CEREDIGION
Wye
Ystrad Meurig
Strata Florida
Radnor
BUELLT
Teifi
Cardigan
DEHEUBARTH
Cilgerran
Towy
Hay
Hereford
Bronllys
Brecon
ST DAVID'S
Dynevor
BRECKNOCK
Crickhowell
Carmarthen
Haverfordwest
Whitland
Abergavenny
Usk
Monmouth
Cydweli
GWENT
Tenby
Pembroke
Manorbier
GOWER
Neath Abbey
Swansea
Caerleon
Margam
Coity
Talyfan
LLANDAFF
Newport
Ogmore
Ewenni
Cardiff
0 10 20 30 Miles
0 10 20 30 40 Kilometres

A

D Manorbier Castle — a modern photograph.

E A statue of Gerald at St David's.

In one book which told of a journey he made through Wales with Archbishop Baldwin in 1188 Gerald gave a detailed description of his home district. This description F shows Gerald's deep affection for this lovely land, although he spent most of his life far away from it, and far from the castle of his childhood.

F Only about three miles from Pembroke Castle is the fortified mansion known as Manorbier ... There the house stands, visible from afar because of its turrets and crenellations, on the top of a hill which is quite near the sea and which on the western side reaches as far as the harbour. To the north and north-west, just beneath the walls, there is an excellent fishpond, well constructed and remarkable for its deep waters. On the same side there is a most attractive orchard, shut in between the fish-pond and a grove of trees, with a great crag of rock and hazel-nut trees which grow to a great height. At the east end of the fortified promontory, between the castle, if I may call it such, and the church, a stream of water which never fails winds its way along a valley, which is strewn with sand by the strong sea-winds. It runs down from a large lake, and there is a water-mill on its bank. To the west it is washed by a winding inlet of the Severn Sea which forms a bay quite near to the castle and yet looks out towards the Irish Sea. If only the rocky headland to the south bent round northwards a little farther, it would make a harbour most convenient for shipping. Boats on their way to Ireland from almost any part of Britain scud by before the east wind ... This is a region rich in wheat, with fish from the sea and plenty of wine for sale. What is more important than all the rest is that, from its nearness to Ireland, heaven's breath smells so wooingly there.

(Gerald of Wales, *The Journey through Wales*, trans. Lewis Thorpe)

The ruins of Manorbier still stand today, and they can be seen in picture D. This is how the traveller Richard Fenton described the site nearly two centuries ago: G

G The castle remains the most perfect example of a Norman baronial home, with all its additions — a church, a dovecot, ponds, a park and orchard which may be discerned still, and the houses of servants within earshot.

(Richard Fenton, *Tours of Wales*)

2. What did Gerald have to say about the area where he was brought up?

3. Draw a picture of Manorbier castle and the land around it as you suppose it was in Gerald's lifetime. Base the picture on Gerald's own description in extract F. What was it about the castle that appealed to Gerald, considering that the castles of the period were military structures? What advantages did the castle's position have?

The Normans of south Wales were warlike people, just like the Welsh who opposed them. Gerald and his brothers were raised on tales of war and fighting. He had three older brothers: Walter, Robert and Philip. In 1169 two of them sailed with a 'private army', drawn from among the family of Nest, to conquer part of Ireland. Robert was badly wounded there while storming the castle of Wexford. Gerald heard about the battle while he was a student in Paris. Gerald's taste for strange tales can be seen in this account of his brother's injury:

H Among those who were injured was Robert de Barri, a young soldier fired with fierce bravery, and he was among the first to scale the walls, fearless in the face of death; but he was struck on the helm by a great boulder, and he fell headlong into the ditch below, scarcely alive — his comrades had great difficulty in pulling him out. Sixteen years later his eye-teeth all fell out as a result of this blow, and stranger still, new teeth grew to replace them.

(Gerald of Wales, *Expugnatio Hibernica*)

4. What happened to Robert de Barri at Wexford?

3. THE STUDENT AND THE PRIEST

GERALD'S CHILDHOOD

Let us look at Gerald's family life through his own words. Around 1208 he began to write out his autobiography — his life story — in full. He completed some 19 chapters, and he wrote rough headings for about 200 more, but he probably never finished those. An extract from that book, *De Rebus a Se Gestis* ('About his Deeds') follows next. In it he remembers his brothers and himself as children: A

A ... when the other three, preluding the pursuits of manhood in their childish play, were tracing or building, in sand or dust, now towns, now palaces, he himself, in like prophetic play, was ever busy with all his might in designing churches or building monasteries. And his father, who often saw him thus engaged, after much pondering, not unmixed with wonder, being moved by this omen, resolved with wise forethought to set him to study letters and the liberal **arts**, and would oft in approving jest call him 'his bishop'.

(Gerald of Wales, *De Rebus a Se Gestis*, trans. H. E. Butler)

B Soldiers attacking a castle.

Did you notice something unusual about that extract, in view of the fact that Gerald himself was telling the story? Usually, in an autobiography, the author writes 'I did this ...', or 'I said ...', but in Gerald's autobiography you can see that he writes 'He did this ...', 'He said ...' and so on. This happens through most of his work. Whenever he refers to himself he does so as if he were describing someone else — 'the author' or 'Giraldus'; he rarely uses words like 'my ...', 'me ...' or 'I'.

Gerald tells one exciting story about his childhood which shows how dangerous an age this was in Welsh history. Again, see how he refers to himself as 'the boy' or 'the child': C

C Now it happened that one night, when the country was disturbed by a raid of the enemy, and all the young men of the castle sprang to arms, the boy on seeing this and hearing the tumult burst into tears and, seeking some place of safety, begged that he might be carried to the church, thus with marvellous foreknowledge proclaiming that the peace of the church and the sanctuary of God's house should be the strongest and most secure place of refuge; and in truth all that heard of this thing ... called to mind with wonder that he promised greater safety for himself in a lonely church exposed to all the winds and to the strokes of chance than in a town filled with men-at-arms and strongly fortified with walls and towers.

(Gerald of Wales, *De Rebus a Se Gestis*, trans. H. E. Butler)

1. What made Gerald's father think of arranging a career in the Church for his son?

Although his heart was set on the Church early on, he was not so ready to spend his time studying hard to become a priest — at least, not at first. Gerald wrote that playing with his brothers or watching them at their weapons' training often distracted him from his studies. But his uncle told him off. This uncle was David, Bishop of St David's — the oldest and most important **diocese** in Wales. David sent two priests to be Gerald's teachers. They made fun of him so mercilessly for failing to learn Latin that the boy decided to take the work seriously.

2. What kind of childhood did Gerald have, in your opinion? Would any of these descriptions be suitable: (a) quiet and peaceful; (b) boring and uneventful; (c) exciting and dangerous?

When he grew older Gerald was sent to the great monastery of St Peter's at Gloucester, where he was taught by Master Hamo — a very learned monk who had spent his life reading, studying and teaching young people. In those days boys training to be priests were not the only ones taught by the monks. Monks and priests were almost the only people who took on the tasks of studying and teaching others professionally. Copies of books were usually made in the monasteries. At that time, before the printing press had been invented, the only way to get a new copy of a book was to write it out by hand, word for word, with a quill-pen and ink. It might take years to complete a copy of a large book, and often more than one copyist would work on different parts of it. Libraries and the knowledge contained in books, were mainly in the possession of priests and monks. These people, then, were the only ones who could teach the children of the lords and knights. All schools and universities were run by clergymen.

D A monk writing out a book.

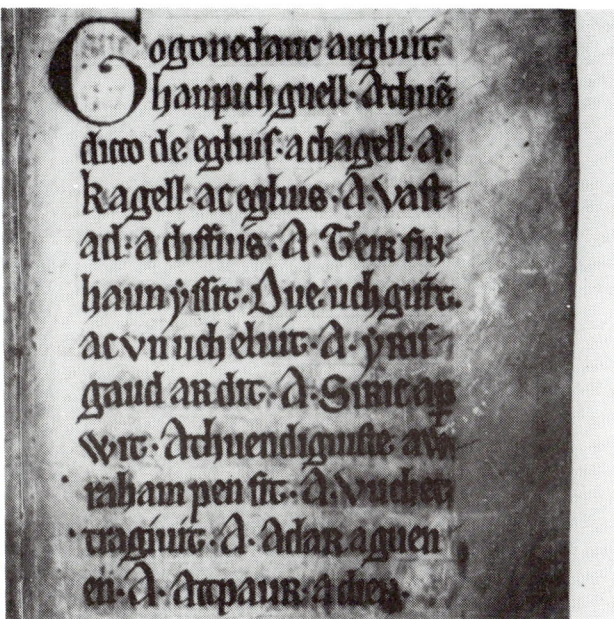

E A page from the Black Book of Carmarthen, written in the Middle Ages.

Gerald went to the University of Paris after his time at Gloucester. He spent several years there. Here is his own story of his student days: F

F ... he was so wholly devoted to his studies, and so free from all levity and frivolity both in word and deed that, as often as the teachers of the Arts desired to produce a pattern of excellence from among their best scholars, with one accord they named Giraldus in preference to all the rest. And thus in the first years of his youth his merits made him worthy not merely to seek but also to set an example of excellence in the duties of a scholar.

(Gerald of Wales, *De Rebus a Se Gestis*, trans. H. E. Butler)

3. What kind of student was Gerald, according to his own account?

You'll have seen that Gerald was not too modest about his successes! This self-confidence strengthened him for a life of difficulties, but it made enemies for him too.

4. Where was Gerald educated?

5. What words would you use to give your opinion about Gerald as his own description in extract F shows him?

A PRIEST'S LIFE

Gerald returned from France around the year 1174, when he was 28 years old. It was not unusual for a scholar from a wealthy family to spend a very long time studying before taking up a job. On the other hand, Gerald had been no ordinary student. According to his own account he spent some time lecturing too — teaching other students what he had learnt by his own studies.

Gerald became a parish priest as soon as he came home — almost certainly through the influence of his uncle the Bishop of St David's. Indeed Gerald was appointed priest of several parishes at the same time — something which needs explaining. To someone of Gerald's background, and with a burning ambition to make a name for himself in the Church, the **income** he got as the priest of a single parish was far from being enough. The custom of being priest to several parishes at once, called **pluralism**, was very common throughout the Middle Ages and for a long time after. It became a serious problem, in fact. Many parishes were left without a full-time priest. No priest could live in a number of parishes at the same time; so parish work was neglected and a **curate** would try to fill the gap, being paid a small share of the vicar's income for his efforts.

G A teacher and his pupils in a monastery school.

Gerald saw nothing wrong with being the vicar of the parishes of Angle, Tenby, Llanwnda and Laugharne, all in Dyfed, and Chesterton, Oxfordshire, with other church appointments in Mathry and Hereford. But he was still not satisfied — he never lived in any one of these places! He went to Canterbury — the mother-church of the Roman Catholic Church in Britain, according to its Archbishops. Gerald was given a job by the Archbishop of Canterbury, to make sure that the **tithe** of wool and cheese was paid in full in the diocese of St David's.

The Flemings living in the Rhos district of Pembroke had been excused from paying this tithe for years. They were settlers from the Netherlands who had been brought to Wales by Henry I. This made the Welsh unwilling to pay the tithe too, but Gerald eventually persuaded them to pay.

Although his actions angered some Normans in the diocese, as well as the Flemings, including one knight who threatened to kill him, Gerald had shown that he was a determined and hard-working man. Before long he was promoted in the Church. He had been sent to Brecknock as part of his mission for the Archbishop. There he found that the Archdeacon, an elderly man named Jordan, was married — a serious breach of Church law. Gerald told the old man either to divorce his wife or resign as Archdeacon. Jordan decided to resign, and Gerald was appointed to replace him. So now he was **Archdeacon of Brecknock**.

6. Who, in the diocese of St David's, were least willing to pay the tithe in 1174, and why?

7. How did Gerald become Archdeacon of Brecknock?

8. What problems did people like Gerald cause the Church in the Middle Ages?

9. Do you think getting hold of a copy of a particular book was an easy or a difficult matter in the Middle Ages, and why?

4. FAME AND NO FORTUNE

GERALD AT COURT

Gerald spent some time as an official in the service of two kings — Henry II and his son Richard I. He also helped another of Henry II's sons, who later became King John. Of these three kings there is no doubt that the father, Henry II, made the greatest impression on Gerald. In one modern book about Henry and his sons a novelist wrote about a sharp, witty comment made by someone at court: A

A Giraldus Cambrensis smiles with discreet pleasure. He must remember to fit this spontaneous expression of opinion into the book he is now writing. But then he is always beginning books which, whatever their titles, turn out to be principally concerned with King Henry ...

(Alfred Duggan, *Devil's Brood*)

There is some truth in that statement: Gerald mentioned Henry in many of his books. After all, not many people are able to get to know a king well, or be a fairly important royal official. Picture B shows a number of clergymen greeting their king, Henry II.

B

Gerald's first period in the royal service was in 1184-5. He became a clerk at the king's court, not an unusual step for a talented clergyman in those days. Clergymen were expected to be fluent in Latin and to be able to write letters and record decisions made by the king. Few other people could write more than their names, far less use the international language of Latin. This was the language of most books and official papers — laws, letters and treaties between countries.

1. Why did clergymen make useful royal servants in the Middle Ages?

In 1183, after he had shown everyone in Brecknock that they had a strong and active Archdeacon, Gerald went to Ireland with his brother. Gerald's relatives, along with other Norman knights, had conquered lands in Ireland, and Gerald went to visit these new territories with Philip. The story of Gerald in Ireland is told more fully in the book *Gerald and His World*. In 1185 he visited Ireland again with the king's son, Prince John.

C A statue of Gerald in Cardiff.

Gerald stayed there for about a year the second time. He learnt enough to write two books about the history and geography of Ireland. After returning to his house at Llan-ddew — the official home of the Archdeacon of Brecknock — he settled down to finish the books for which he'd been gathering information. Books, of course, were not printed then; neither were there publishing companies to distribute and sell books, or bookshops as we know them. All the same it was possible for the few people who could read to buy copies of the books they wanted: but they would have to wait until the laborious task of copying them out was finished. The only advertising of books would be done by the author himself. This was Gerald's method: D

D And when in process of time the work was finished and corrected, not wishing to place the candle which he had lit under a **bushel**, but to lift it aloft on a candlestick that it might shine, he determined to read it before a great audience at Oxford, where of all places in England the clergy were most strong and pre-eminent in learning. And since his book was divided into three parts, he gave three consecutive days to the reading, a part being read each day. On the first day he hospitably entertained the poor of the whole town whom he gathered together for the purpose; on the morrow he entertained all the **doctors** of the divers **faculties** and those of their scholars who were best known and best spoken of; and on the third day he entertained the remainder of the scholars together with the knights of the town and a number of the citizens. It was a magnificent and costly achievement ... nor has the present age seen ... the like.

(Gerald of Wales, *De Rebus a Se Gestis*, trans. H. E. Butler)

2. How did Gerald set about advertising his books about Ireland?

GERALD MEETS THE MIGHTY

By 1189 Gerald was much better known at the king's court. Yet this was what he wrote about his years of royal service — words that strike a note of disappointment: E

E When therefore for several years he had rendered faithful service by following the Court and had been of great assistance in the pacification of Wales, none the less on account of his kinship with Rhys ap Gruffudd and other princes of Wales, he received of the King, who enriched and promoted so many unworthy persons, nothing save empty promises void of all truth. Yet in secret the King praised him mightily in the presence of his counsellors and approved his character, his self-restraint, his **modesty** and his fidelity, saying that, if he had not been born in Wales and bound so closely by ties of blood to the magnates of Wales, and more especially to Rhys, he would of his bounty have exalted him by the bestowal of ecclesiastical dignities and rich rewards and would have made him a great man in his kingdom.

(Gerald of Wales, *De Rebus a Se Gestis*, trans. H. E. Butler)

3. Show what phrases in extract E give the impression that Gerald was disappointed after his years of working for the king.

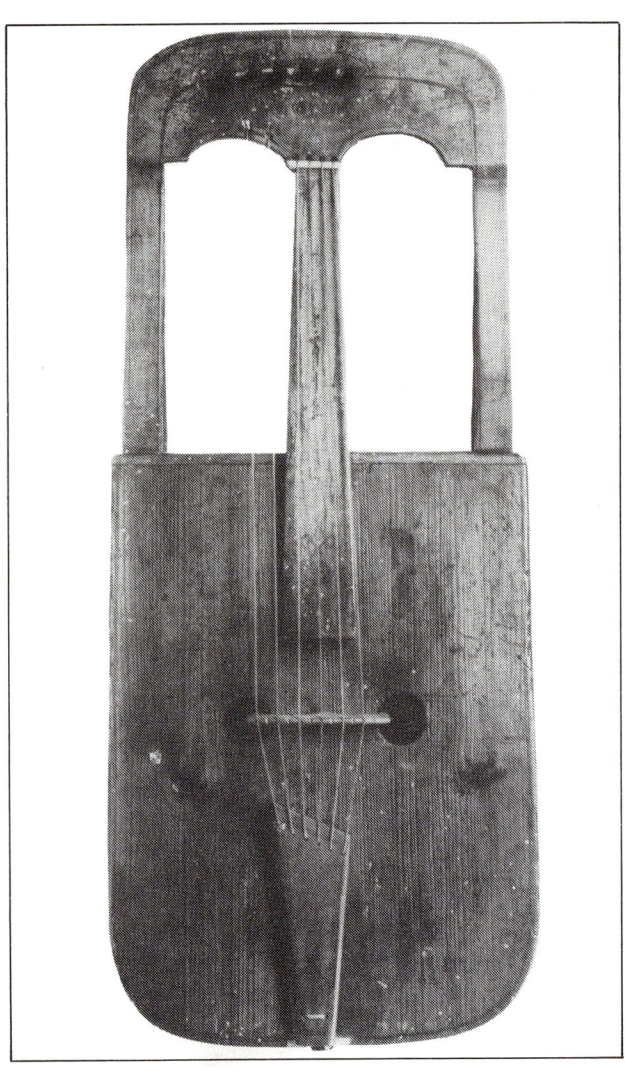

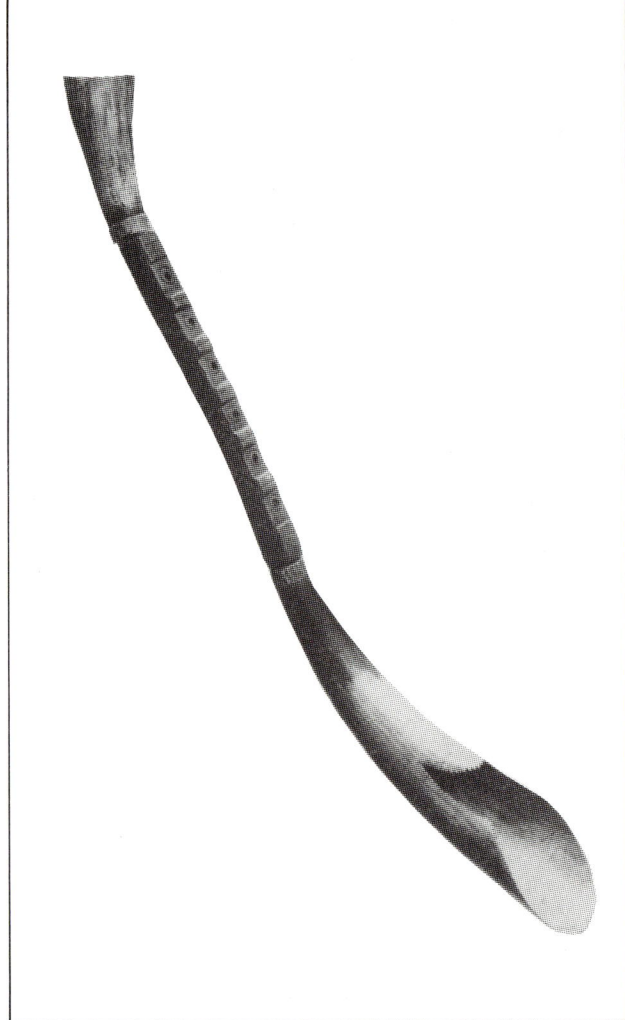

F Musical instruments like these were played in the Middle Ages. Do they look like any modern instruments?

Although Gerald complained that the main obstacle to his promotion was that he was related to the Lord Rhys, it was probably this link that made him useful to the king. The Lord Rhys stood out among the Welsh princes. Here is a story about him from one of the medieval chronicles, *Brut y Tywysogion* — a kind of diary of the great events of the time: G

G 1176 — ... And then the Lord Rhys held a special feast at Cardigan, and he set two kinds of contests: one between the bards and the poets, and another between the harpists and the **crowders** and the pipers and various classes of string-music. And he set two chairs for the victors in the contests. And those he enriched with great gifts. And then a young man from his own court won the victory for string-music. And the men of Gwynedd won the victory for poetry ...

(*Brut y Tywysogion*, trans. Thomas Jones)

4. What kind of contest would this be called in Wales today? What was the importance of the 1176 contest in the history of Wales?

Gerald visited Rhys often on the king's behalf, and he would be part of the king's **retinue** whenever Henry came to Wales — or when Rhys visited the king. Here is Gerald's version of a rather needling conversation between Rhys and himself: H

H And when the Prince was sitting at breakfast in the house of the Bishop of Hereford, William de Vere, ... and he sat between the Bishop and Walter FitzRobert, a noble baron and, like the Bishop, of the house of Clare, Giraldus the Archdeacon drew near and standing before them ... thus addressed Rhys in courteous jest. 'You have cause for rejoicing, O Rhys, and glad you may well be, that here at this feast you sit between two great men of the house of Clare, whose inheritance you hold.' For Rhys then held the whole of the land of Cardigan, which he had recovered from Roger, Earl of Clare. But Rhys, being a man of excellent wit and quick in repartee, at once replied, 'It is true that long since we lost our inheritance to the house of Clare, but since we had to lose it, we are glad to have lost it, not at the hands of sluggards of obscure birth, but to men of such high fame and renown.' The Bishop thereupon added, 'And we too are well pleased, since it was our fate to lose the lands we had possessed so long, that they are now held by so good a man and of such high birth as Rhys.'

(Gerald of Wales, *De Rebus a Se Gestis*, trans. H. E. Butler)

5. What do you think relations had been like between the Lord Rhys' family and the Clare family in the past, according to extract H?

5. THE JOURNEY THROUGH WALES

Since 1095 the Christian kings of Europe had joined forces from time to time in an effort to free Palestine, the ancient homeland of Jesus Christ, from the Turks, a people with a different religion. These wars were known as the Crusades (the wars of the Cross). In 1187 the call went out from the Pope for a third Crusade, and his appeal had reached England and Wales by 1188.

BALDWIN AND GERALD

In 1188 Baldwin, Archbishop of Canterbury, took to the road in an effort to recruit soldiers for the third Crusade, and Gerald went with him. Richard, the king's son, was eager to go to Palestine, and Henry himself sent Baldwin to Wales to rally supporters. The Archbishop's journey began in Hereford. When they reached Radnor Baldwin and his followers met the Lord Rhys, ruler of Deheubarth, and other prominent men. After Baldwin had preached a stirring sermon about the Crusade, the first to step forward to 'take the Cross', or promise to go on Crusade, was Gerald himself. It was a very dramatic scene, but in fact the king had urged Gerald beforehand to come forward, so that others would be spurred on to do the same. Peter de Leia, Bishop of St David's, came forward too, and the flow of volunteers for the Crusade began.

ON THE ROAD IN WALES

The journey through Wales took place during Lent 1188. Lent, in the Church calendar, is a period of fasting and prayer leading up to Easter. At this time of year, in March and April, Baldwin and Gerald made their trip. You can follow their route on map A on page 14. From Radnor the party crossed the River Wye and came to Hay-on-Wye: B

B We crossed the River Wye and made our way into Brecknockshire. After the sermon which was given in Hay, we saw a great number of men who wanted to take the Cross come running towards the castle where the Archbishop was, leaving their cloaks behind in the hands of the wives and friends who had tried to hold them back.

(Gerald of Wales, *Itinerarium Kambriae* ('The Journey through Wales'), trans. Lewis Thorpe)

1. What was the response of the men of Hay to the appeal by Archbishop Baldwin and Gerald?

A

2. Draw an outline copy of map A, to the same scale as in the book, on an A4-sized sheet of drawing paper. Draw in and label the rivers and write in the divisions (e.g. Gwent, Gwynedd). When you have read this whole chapter, note the places Gerald visited on your own copy of the map. Then draw a route-line in a striking colour linking all these places, and tracing the route through Wales. Now draw 6 sketches in the space around your map, each one illustrating a scene from the journey, with an arrow pointing from each sketch to the place it shows on the map.

After resting at Gerald's house in Llan-ddew they visited Brecon, and then went on to Abergavenny through the forest of Coed Grwyne, passing close to Llanthony priory. They visited Usk Castle in Gwent, and William, Bishop of Llandaff, turned up to accompany them through his diocese. At Caerleon Gerald marvelled at the Roman remains to be seen there. Newport and Cardiff were on the route too, and sermons for both the Welsh and English were given in Llandaff cathedral. The Norman castle at Cardiff can be seen in picture D.

Once past the great abbey of Margam they came to some difficult terrain, with dangerous marshes, around the Afan and Neath rivers: C

C As we approached the Neath, which is the most dangerous and difficult of access of all the rivers of South Wales, on account of its quicksands, which immediately engulf anything placed upon them, one of our pack-horses, the only one possessed by the writer of these lines, was almost sucked down into the abyss, ... In the end it was pulled out with some difficulty, thanks to the efforts made by our servants, who risked their lives in doing so, and not without some damage done to my books and baggage.

(Gerald of Wales, *Itinerarium Kambriae*, trans. Lewis Thorpe)

3. What can you judge about travelling conditions in Gerald's day from this account?

D The Norman castle at Cardiff.

More volunteers were recruited in Swansea, before crossing the River Loughor to reach Cydweli. On they went, crossing the River Tywi by boat and eventually reaching Carmarthen. They moved on from there to Whitland abbey.

After crossing the River Taf and the two Cleddau rivers they travelled on to Haverfordwest: E

E In Haverfordwest the Archbishop himself first gave a sermon, and then the word of God was preached with some eloquence by the Archdeacon ... A great crowd of people assembled, some of them soldiers, others civilians. Many found it odd ... that when I, the Archdeacon, preached the word of God, speaking first in Latin and then in French, those who could not understand either language were just as much moved to tears as the others, rushing forward in equal numbers to receive the sign of the Cross.

(Gerald of Wales, *Itinerarium Kambriae*, trans. Lewis Thorpe)

4. Does anything in extract E suggest that Gerald was not very fluent in Welsh?

A welcome awaited them at St David's, where they were the guests of Bishop Peter. Then they moved on through Cardigan, up the Teifi valley to Lampeter and to Strata Florida abbey. The abbot of Strata Florida accompanied them to Llanbadarn, then over the River Dyfi (the farthest limit of the kingdom of Deheubarth), and on to Tywyn in Meirionnydd. The Lord Rhys and Bishop Peter now turned back. From here on the party was accompanied by Gruffudd ap Cynan, the lord of this district which was part of Gwynedd and of the diocese of Bangor.

F Part of the Bishop's palace at St David's. The buildings to be seen there today were built, almost entirely, after Gerald's time.

In crossing from south to north Wales Gerald made this comment on the way Welsh was spoken in the two regions: **G**

G It is thought that the Welsh language is richer, more carefully pronounced and preferable in all respects in North Wales, for that area has far fewer foreigners. Others maintain that the speech of Cardiganshire in South Wales is better articulated and more to be admired, since it is in the middle and the heartland of Wales. In both Cornwall and Brittany they speak almost the same language as in Wales. It comes from the same root and is intelligible to the Welsh in many instances, and almost in all. It is rougher and less clearly pronounced, but probably closer to the original British speech, or so I think myself.

(Gerald of Wales, *Descriptio Kambriae* 'Description of Wales', trans. Lewis Thorpe)

Gerald's account mentions crossing the rivers Dysynni, Mawddach and Artro, and staying overnight at Llanfair, near Harlech. He marvelled at the long spears carried by the northern Welsh, claiming that they used them as effectively as the southern Welsh used the bow.

Leaving Llanfair behind they crossed Traeth Bychan and Traeth Mawr estuaries, and went on through Eifionydd to Llŷn, arriving in Nefyn. After resting and gaining more recruits there, they started for Caernarfon. Gerald wrote briefly about Bardsey Island, a place of pilgrimage for centuries, although neither he nor his companions actually visited the island: **H**

H Beyond Lleyn there is a small island occupied by some extremely devout monks ... Either because of its pure air, which comes across the sea from Ireland, or through some miracle occasioned by the merits of the holy men who live there, the island has this peculiarity, that no one dies there except in extreme old age, for disease is almost unheard of. In fact no one dies there at all, unless he is very old indeed ... The bodies of a vast number of holy men are buried there, or so they say, among them that of Daniel, Bishop of Bangor.

(Gerald of Wales, *Itinerarium Kambriae*, trans. Lewis Thorpe)

When they got to Bangor they found that Gwion, its Bishop, was reluctant to take the Cross, and he had to be forced. He may have been unhappy about accepting the authority of the Archbishop of Canterbury, because Gwynedd was largely independent of the English crown. From Bangor they crossed the Menai Straits to Anglesey, but the response there too was suspicious at first. Rhodri, one of the sons of Owain Gwynedd, scorned every appeal at first, and his followers did the same: **J**

J It came to pass within three days, as if by divine vengeance, that these very same young men, with many others, set off in pursuit of a local band of robbers. The thieves beat them and put them to flight, some being killed there and then, and others mortally wounded. The Cross which they had previously scorned they now of their own free will marked on their own bodies.

(Gerald of Wales, *Itinerarium Kambriae*, trans. Lewis Thorpe)

5. What made Rhodri ap Owain and his friends change their minds about the Crusade?

From Anglesey Baldwin's party returned to Bangor and continued along the coast to Aberconwy, crossing the estuary by boat. The new abbey at Aberconwy may have been under construction then. It was to be moved up the Conwy valley to Maenan after 1282, when Edward I decided to build Conwy Castle on its site. On they travelled from Aberconwy to Rhuddlan Castle. Dafydd, another son of Owain Gwynedd, was the ruler here, on the banks of the River Clwyd. Picture **K** shows the English castle built there many years later.

I Bardsey Island.

K Rhuddlan Castle — built after 1277 close to the site of Dafydd ab Owain's castle, originally built by the Normans.

Baldwin held the service of **mass** in St Asaph cathedral, the last of the Welsh cathedrals the party visited. They carried on through northern Clwyd, known as Tegeingl in Gerald's time, and they stayed the night at the small abbey of Basingwerk. Perilous marshes faced them again along the Dee estuary as they approached Chester. They arrived there two days before Easter. After celebrating Easter in Chester, they started off once more.

They passed Whitchurch and Oswestry and came to the borders of the principality of Powys. In Shrewsbury, near journey's end, Archbishop Baldwin **excommunicated** Owain Cyfeiliog, prince of Powys. He was the only one of the Welsh princes who had not come to meet the Archbishop. Gerald gave this description of Owain Cyfeiliog: L

L This Owain was much more fluent in speech than the other Welsh princes and he was well known for the sensible way in which he managed his land. He had frequently opposed the plans of his own leaders and had espoused the cause of Henry II, King of the English.

(Gerald of Wales, *Itinerarium Kambriae*, trans. Lewis Thorpe)

M Shrewsbury today.

Another unusual fact about Owain Cyfeiliog was that he was the only poet among the princes of Wales at that time. Most of the Welsh princes and lords took an interest in poetry, because the poets who lived at their courts were there to sing the praises of the lords and their families. Lords who could compose poetry themselves, however, were rare.

From Shrewsbury they moved on to Wenlock, Bishop Peter's old **priory**. At one stage they had to make their way along a dangerous ridge — it was

N Wenlock Priory today.

called the Malpas ('Bad Way') — then onwards, through the Welsh **Marches**, past Ludlow and Leominster to end their journey at Hereford.

The journey through Wales had taken some seven weeks in all, and Gerald claimed that 3,000 men were recruited for the Crusade as a result.

Not all these people went to the Middle East, however. Gerald himself, you remember, had been the first to 'take the Cross' at Radnor, but he never went to war. Many were released from their promise on condition that they gave a sum of money towards the cost of the war and did something to improve the state of the Church in their own area. Archbishop Baldwin himself went to the Middle East and died on the Crusade.

6. How many Welsh rivers are named in this chapter? Why did Gerald keep mentioning the rivers?

7. Why was Bishop Gwion unwilling to 'take the Cross'?

8. What, according to Gerald, was the favourite weapon of the men of North Wales and what was the favourite of the South Wales men?

9. What differences did Gerald find between the Welsh spoken in different parts of Wales?

10. Try to find out what the Welsh names are for these places which Gerald visited on the 1188 journey: St David's, Cardiff, Cardigan, Anglesey, Brecon, St Asaph.

6. TRIUMPH AND DEFEAT

After Henry II died in 1189 Gerald joined the court of the new king, Richard I. Richard was a courageous soldier. He soon had England under firm control, but in his French lands there was further war and bloodshed.

Even before the new king had been crowned he sent Gerald from France to Wales with important letters. Gerald nearly lost these letters, all his money and the only manuscript of *Itinerarium Kambriae* ('The Journey through Wales') on the way from Dieppe to Abbeville. He and his servant lost each other as they forded an estuary, and although Gerald had given up hope of ever seeing the man again, he turned up one night at Gerald's lodgings in Abbeville. Gerald was delighted to see him — and all the baggage he had been carrying. The servant had got into difficulties crossing the estuary and later had to stop to repair his horse's harness.

GERALD AND HUBERT WALTER

After 1193 Richard left the work of ruling the kingdom to Hubert Walter, Archbishop of Canterbury. Gerald disliked him deeply, and he made this known in one of his books. Of course this angered the Archbishop and there was little chance that he would promote Gerald to a more important job after that!

Gerald left the king's service and went back to studying. He spent some time in Hereford, and then settled in Lincoln, leaving his archdeaconry in Brecknock in the care of a local clergyman. Not everyone at court had turned against him. Prince John, who had known him since the visit to Ireland years before, was still friendly. Gerald was offered the chance of becoming Bishop of Bangor and of Llandaff during this period, but he turned down both offers.

A King Richard I (1189-99).

Gerald longed to return to the University of Paris, where he had once been a student and a teacher; but it was not to be. He could not risk going to Paris because of the fighting in France, so he went to Lincoln instead. He had been a successful priest and scholar, and for a time even a promising **politician**: but the days of his greatest fame were yet to come.

B A chained library. What does this picture suggest about books in the Middle Ages?

THE DIOCESE OF ST DAVID'S

In July 1198 Peter de Leia, Bishop of St David's, died. Although Peter had been Bishop since 1176, he had not lived all that time at St David's. He ended his days in Tewkesbury Abbey. Gerald had been appointed to look after the diocese on Peter's behalf from 1179 to 1183, but since then there had been hostility between them. Yet it was during Peter's time that work began on the building of a new cathedral which is still a place of worship to this day. C Peter's death gave Gerald another chance of becoming Bishop of St David's.

The ill-feeling between the two men had grown worse in the 1190s, after a quarrel between Peter and the sons of the Lord Rhys. Peter was taken **hostage** by the sons, and after his release he **excommunicated** them — and their father too. Rhys died while he was still excommunicated, a dreaded fate in those days. When the sons vowed revenge against Peter, he in turn tried to blame Gerald for giving him bad advice. Soon afterwards Peter began to keep the income from Gerald's churches for himself, and Gerald appealed to the Pope. This dispute was still smouldering when Peter died.

1. What were relations like between Gerald and Bishop Peter of St David's between 1176 and 1198?

[C] St David's Cathedral.

On 29 June 1199 Gerald was elected Bishop of St David's from a list of four candidates drawn up the previous September. But both the King and the Pope wanted a share in the decision, so the election at St David's was only the beginning of the struggle to make Gerald its bishop.

Gerald believed St David's had been chosen to be Wales' most important church centuries earlier, and that St David himself had been Archbishop of all Wales. If St David's was an archbishopric, control of Wales' other dioceses should be ruled from there, and not from Canterbury, the 'mother-church' of England.

In Gwynedd the boy-warrior Llywelyn ap Iorwerth had grown into a powerful and determined prince. Perhaps Welshmen like Llywelyn might be prepared to support a bid to free the Welsh Church from that of England.

2. Why was St David's a special diocese in Gerald's view?

GERALD'S STRUGGLE

Gerald's name had been put on a list of names to be considered for the bishopric of St David's in 1198. Such a list would be drawn up by Canons, or the leading clergymen of the diocese. Gerald was the Canons' choice, but Geoffrey FitzPeter, the King's Justiciar (chief officer) and Hubert Walter, Archbishop of Canterbury, were opposed to all four candidates. The case was sent before the king, who was fighting in France at the time. Two priests went over to France, but when they arrived they heard that King Richard had been killed, and that John was now king. John supported Gerald at first — after all he had known him for many years. But by the time he returned to England and was crowned, Hubert Walter and others had persuaded him that Gerald might be dangerous as Bishop of St David's. The Canons, however, were backing Gerald so strongly that they went ahead on their own to elect him Bishop, without permission from Canterbury or from the king: [D] on page 20.

D The Archdeacon therefore considering the grievous desolation of his Church through its lack of a shepherd, and how its ancient right had almost been lost for ever by reason of long silence, reflecting also how the desires of all the clergy and people were alike centred upon him ... for all these reasons abandoned his firm-set purpose and his most blessed life of study, and at length ... gave his consent. And forthwith such courage and heart grew within him that he delivered himself up without hesitation or delay to the task of re-establishing the former state of his Church and with it the honour of his country as though he had been born and appointed by God for this purpose.

(Gerald of Wales, *De Rebus a Se Gestis*, trans. H. E. Butler)

3. Which words of Gerald's in this extract explain why he accepted the plea of the St David's canons in 1199? Write out those words.

Gerald was now in a very insecure position. He had been elected by the canons on 29 June 1199 — but against the wishes of the king and Hubert Walter. At St David's he was welcomed warmly. He carried out the work of a Bishop and he was respected as if he were the Bishop; but he had not been consecrated, and so he was not yet a full Bishop in the eyes of the Catholic Church. The only way to overcome opposition to him in London and Canterbury was to ask the Pope in Rome to confirm his election. That is just what Gerald did.

4. Gerald was said to be 'in a very insecure position' in 1199. Why?

E Pope Innocent III.

Gerald went to Rome himself, taking with him a letter from the Canons of St David's. Innocent III was the Pope at that time, and Gerald gave him six of the books he had written as a gift: **F**

F Now the Pope, who was most learned and loved literature, kept all these books together by his bedside for about a month and used to display their elegant and pithy phrases to the Cardinals who visited him, and finally gave all save one to different Cardinals who asked for them. But the *Gemma Ecclesiastica* ('The Jewel of the Church'), which he loved beyond the rest, he would not suffer to be parted from.

(Gerald of Wales, *De Rebus a Se Gestis*, trans. H. E. Butler)

In all fairness to Gerald, when he wrote his own life-story he did not leave out the letter that Hubert Walter had sent to the Pope — a letter that said harsh things about Gerald and the way he had been elected Bishop of St David's. Here is a part of that letter: **G**

G Most Holy Father, I do not think that you are ignorant that the Church of Canterbury is the Mother and Metropolis of the Church of Mynyw [St David's] and the other Churches of all Wales; ... None the less, of late ... a certain Archdeacon of the Church of Mynyw, Giraldus by name, a Welshman by nation and the kinsman by blood or affinity of many of the magnates of Wales ... has procured his election to the Bishopric of Mynyw by the voice of three Canons only, whom (it is said) he had induced thereto in a manner far from right or seemly, though none of the other Canons showed him favour or gave their assent. Yet he, relying on such a nomination, has not sought or waited for the boon of confirmation by myself, to whom first he should have had recourse ...

(Gerald of Wales, *De Rebus a Se Gestis*, trans. H. E. Butler)

The arguments echoed back and forth for nearly four years. Hubert claimed that Gerald had made 'bloody threats' against one Canon who had opposed him. Gerald said that Hubert was against him because he was Welsh; and if a Welshman could not be a Bishop in Wales, 'no Englishmen should be bishops in England, or Frenchmen in France, or Italians in Italy.'

After all the trouble and the travelling, the probing and the persuading, the sending and answering of letters, Gerald was finally defeated.

DEFEAT AND DISAPPOINTMENT

Hubert Walter persuaded the Canons of St David's to accept Geoffrey of Henlaw, the head of Llanthony Priory (picture **H**) as their Bishop, in the event of Gerald's appeal being turned down by the

H Llanthony Priory in the shadow of the hills.

Pope. He, like Gerald, had been born in the diocese, and by 1202 Gerald could see that he was losing the support of his own clergy. Yet the Pope supported him, he reckoned. Gerald returned to Rome early in 1203, his hopes high, to hear the results of a commission of enquiry set up the last time he was there.

On 10 April 1203 the Pope announced that Gerald had not been elected Bishop in a correct and proper way. Therefore he was not the rightful Bishop of St David's. Pope Innocent did not give his verdict on the status of St David's — whether it was an Archbishopric or not. That question would be settled some other time, he promised.

GERALD GIVES UP

Gerald was very short of money by this time. Moneylenders trooped after him, pestering him to repay his debts. The last time he had been to Wales he could hardly find anyone to give him shelter. Old friends had turned their backs on him, churches and abbeys had closed their doors to him, and he was forced to wander around the countryside alone like an outlaw on the run. His only supporters now were the Welsh princes — Llywelyn ap Iorwerth and the sons of Rhys — but the Welsh priests were more dependent on Hubert Walter and the king than on them.

Although the Pope had put the diocese of St David's in Gerald's charge until a new election could be held, Gerald knew that the battle was lost. The international situation had done more than anything else to swing the Pope's judgement against Gerald. The ambitious Innocent III was in conflict with other leaders in Europe and he could not afford to annoy King John too — supporting Gerald would have done just that.

Later in 1203 Gerald agreed that Geoffrey of Henlaw should become Bishop of St David's. Hubert Walter seized this chance of settling the dispute once and for all. Between November 1203 and early 1204 he got Gerald to agree to Geoffrey's election, to promise never to raise the matter of St David's status again and to resign as Archdeacon of Brecknock. The Archbishop sealed this package of promises by agreeing to put forward Gerald's nephew for the Archdeaconry of Brecknock. The Pope had ordered that the costs of Gerald's long campaign should be paid by the Church, and the Archbishop agreed.

5. What were the terms of the agreement made between Gerald and Hubert Walter in 1203-4?

6. Try to find out more about the Popes in Rome, and make a fact-sheet out of the details you have discovered.

7. Why, do you think, would a Welsh prince like Llywelyn ap Iorwerth find it useful to have Gerald as an Archbishop at St David's?

7. THE TWILIGHT YEARS

GERALD IN OLD AGE

After 1203 Gerald went to Lincoln to live among his books. His life there might have been quiet and content but for the activities of his own nephew — also named Gerald. The older Gerald, you remember, had arranged for his nephew to become Archdeacon of Brecknock, but he himself was to manage the Archdeaconry's business and income. The nephew and his tutor, William di Capella, plotted to wrench this control from Gerald's hands. Bishop Geoffrey at St David's seems to have helped them to do so. Gerald was enraged, and he wrote a book full of savage bitterness to describe the nephew and his tutor — *Speculum Duorum* ('The Mirror of Two Men') — a mirror which reflected two rather shabby characters. Here is part of Gerald's criticism of his nephew: [A]

[A] You wrote to us that it was because of lack of horses that you were unable to come to us at the appointed time as you promised. However, you were sufficiently well provided with horses to go to St David's, Mathry, and Cardigan to perpetrate your acts of treachery. Yet you could not get horses to return to Lincoln ... You even asked us to send you horses, but those which we provided for you on your departure, you very politely returned, covered with sores as a result of neglect — I would almost say by intention — and suffering from starvation. (This is not surprising, since you sent the horses back without fodder, and the stable-lads without travelling money; and those men we had specially sent from Lincoln to Wales, who had worked faithfully for you through the harvest, gathering and stacking the corn, you sent back without their rightful wages or even expenses for the return!).

(Gerald of Wales, *Speculum Duorum,* trans. B. Dawson)

And this is what he wrote about the tutor, William di Capella: [B]

[B] We also saved his life when those youths from Kinnersley drew their swords and attacked him in our presence. We also had his horse worth three or four marks, as well as his sword, which this great fighter, this extraordinary swordsman, had immediately handed over to his enemies, and his cap and equipment returned to him intact ...

His criminality first came to light in the case of their [the Kinnersley youths'] nephew, then a youth, the parson of the church of Kinnersley whom he dishonestly deceived and cozened ... This is the way he acquired everything he has, since he acquired the church at Llanhamlach, as has been said, by bastardized schedules, by false witnesses, and clear perjury.

(Gerald of Wales, *Speculum Duorum*, trans. Brian Dawson)

1. What was the original cause of the quarrel between Gerald and his nephew, which took place around 1207?

2. Draw a strip cartoon telling the story of the troubles Gerald's nephew and the tutor encountered on the road.

[C] Part of a page of *Speculum Duorum*: it is possible that the notes in the margin are in Gerald's own handwriting.

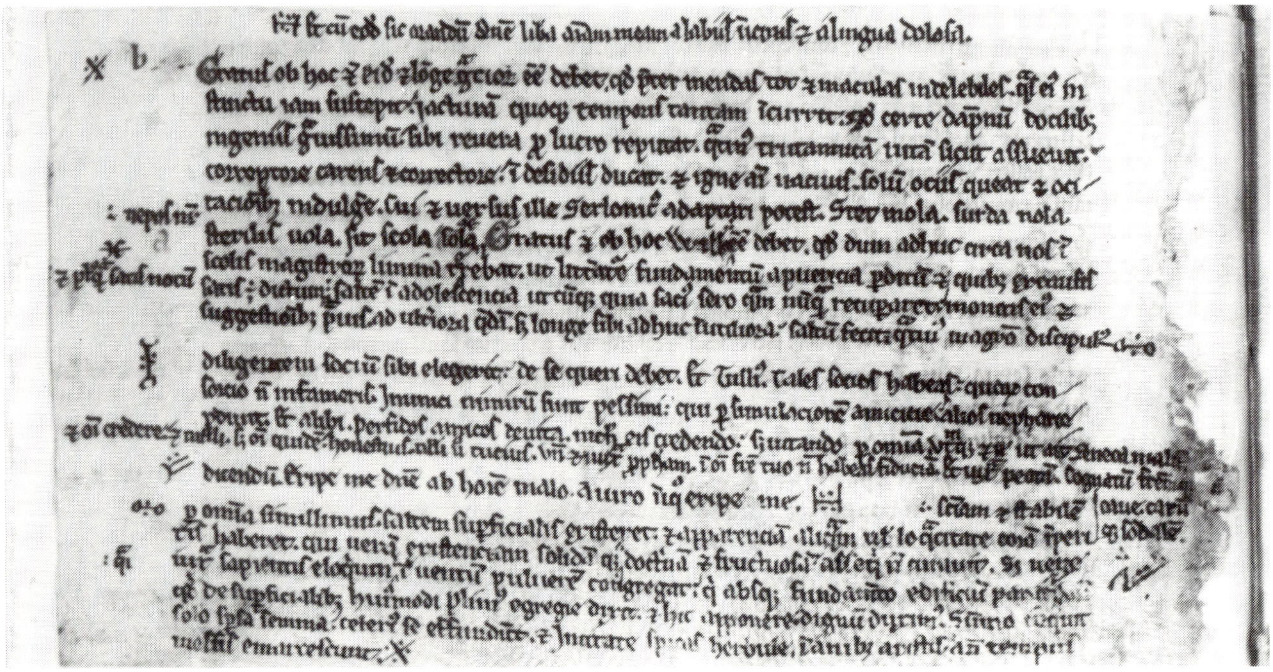

THE LAST YEARS

Gerald spent the rest of his life in Lincoln, but even there, as an old man, excitement followed him. King John's quarrel with his leading lords was growing worse, and in 1215 he was forced to agree to a charter of rights for his people — Magna Carta. He soon began to ignore the charter, and some of his own lords joined an invading French army brought over to England by Prince Louis, the son of King Philip Augustus of France. War raged between England and France in 1216-17, although King John himself died late in 1216. The English lords then united against the French, and Lincoln was one of the last places the French surrendered before they were driven out of England in 1217. It is possible that Gerald may have supported John's enemies during the civil war — one of his books suggests that. He suffered no punishment, however, and he died peacefully around March 1223. He is believed to have been buried at St David's.

Here is the verdict of a German scholar, Michael Richter, on Gerald of Wales after studying his life and his writings: D

D Welsh history in the Middle Ages is the history of a country which was slowly being conquered and reshaped by a strong and determined neighbour. Few great personalities stand out who attempted to stem this development, but certainly Giraldus must be named side by side with the two Llywelyns and Owen Glyn Dŵr. The greatness of three of these lies in their political ideas and actions. Giraldus, however, will be remembered for his individual contribution. His career full of setbacks and without eventual fulfilment in public life moved him to write copiously about himself and the country in which he was born. Giraldus is the greatest writer in Latin whom Wales has ever produced. It is mainly in this sense that he will be appreciated as Giraldus Cambrensis [Gerald of Wales].

(Michael Richter, *Giraldus Cambrensis*)

3. The historian, Michael Richter, compares Gerald with Welsh heroes such as Llywelyn the Great, Llywelyn ap Gruffudd and Owain Glyndŵr. Try to find out more about these other heroes, and decide whether you agree with Michael Richter or not.

Date	English Title	Latin Title
1188	The Conquest of Ireland	*Expugnatio Hibernica*
1188	The Topography of Ireland	*Topographia Hibernica*
1191	The Journey through Wales	*Itinerarium Kambriae*
1194	The Description of Wales	*Descriptio Kambriae*
1194	The Life of St David, Archbishop of Mynyw	*De Vita Sancti Davidis Menuensis Archiepiscopi*
1195	The Life of Godfrey, Archbishop of York	*De Vita Galfridi, Archiepiscopi Ebroacensis*
1197	The Jewel of the Church	*Gemma Ecclesiastica*
1203	About his Activities	*De Rebus a Se Gestis*
1216	About his Defamation	*De Invectionibus*
1216	The Mirror of Two Men	*Speculum Duorum*
1218	About the Authority and Status of the Church of Mynyw	*De Iure et Statu Menuensis Ecclesiae*

E Gerald's most important books.

F Writing a book in the Middle Ages.

8. GLOSSARY

Archdeacon — an important clergyman, on the next rung down from a bishop, and with a wide area in his care.

Arts — subjects like history, literature, languages and religious education are 'arts' subjects in schools and colleges today. Public debating was included in Gerald's day as well, but not design or graphic art.

Bushel — a large container or storage dish.

Crowder — a musician who plays a medieval string-instrument known as the 'crwth'.

Curate — a clergyman who assists a parish priest.

Diocese — a district whose churches are all controlled by a single bishop.

Doctors — people with doctors' degrees from a university: not necessarily medical degrees. It is possible to take a doctor's degree in most academic subjects.

Excommunicate — to exclude someone from membership and from the services of the Church.

Faculties — the teachers of a group of related subjects in a school or university.

Family Tree (Genealogy) — a diagram or list showing how the members of a family are related to each other over several generations.

Hostage — someone who is held prisoner in order to put pressure on others to take some action or pay money to get that person released.

Income — the money a parish priest received, not in wages, but in fees for burials, baptisms and weddings, as well as the tithe.

Marches — the independent lordships in south and east Wales and on the English border from the Norman period up to the age of Henry VIII.

Mass — the most important religious service in the Roman Catholic Church: receiving the bread and wine (the body and blood of Jesus Christ).

Modesty — being reluctant to praise your own work, and seeing other people as more important than yourself. Is this a good description of Gerald?

Pluralism — holding more than one full-time job at the same time.

Politician — someone who takes part in the work of running a country or locality, or who is trying to get elected to do that work — a member of parliament or a councillor.

Priory — a lesser monastery.

Retinue — the officials, guards and servants who travelled with a king or some other important person.

Tithe — ten per cent of the produce of every farm in a parish: it was usually paid to the priest every year as part of his income.